SYMBOLON
THE CATHOLIC FAITH EXPLAINED

Part 1
Knowing the Faith

Participant's Guide

Sessions 1-10

Dr. Edward Sri
General Editor

Nihil Obstat: Ben Akers, S.T.L. and Alphonso L Pinto, M.A., S.T.D.
Imprimatur: Most Reverend Samuel J. Aquila, S.T.L., Archbishop of Denver
August 1, 2013 and March 2016

Copyright © 2014/2016 Augustine Institute. All rights reserved.
With the exception of short excerpts used in articles and critical reviews, no part of this work may be reproduced, transmitted, or stored in any form whatsoever, printed or electronic, without the prior permission of the publisher.

Excerpts from the Lectionary for Mass for Use in the Dioceses of the United States of America, second typical edition © 2001, 1998, 1997, 1986, 1970 Confraternity of Christian Doctrine, Inc., Washington, D.C. Used with permission. All rights reserved. No portion of this text may be reproduced by any means without permission in writing from the copyright owner.

Some Scripture verses contained herein are from the Catholic Edition of the Revised Standard Version of the Bible, copyright ©1965, 1966 by the Division of Christian Educators of the National Council of the Churches of Christ in the United States of America. Used by permission. All rights reserved.

English translation of the *Catechism of the Catholic Church* for the United States of America, copyright ©1994, United States Catholic Conference, Inc.—Libreria Editrice Vaticana. English translation of the *Catechism of the Catholic Church: Modification from the Editio Typica* copyright ©1997, United States Catholic Conference, Inc.—Libreria Editrice Vaticana.

Writers: Woodeene Koenig-Bricker, Lucas Pollice, Dr. Edward Sri

Media/Print Production: Brenda Kraft, Justin Leddick, Kevin Mallory, John Schmidt

Graphic Design: Stacy Innerst, Jane Myers, Nicole Skorka, Jeffrey Wright

ACKNOWLEDGMENT

We would like to acknowledge with heartfelt gratitude the many catechists, teachers, and diocesan leaders from across the country that have given invaluable advice and guidance in the development of Symbolon:

Michael Andrews, Keith Borchers, Steve Bozza, Dr. Chris Burgwald, James Cavanagh, Chris Chapman, Fr. Dennis Gill, Jim Gontis, Dr. Tim Gray, Lisa Gulino, Mary Hanbury, Deacon Ray Helgeson, Dr. Sean Innerst, Ann Lankford, Deacon Kurt Lucas, Sean Martin, Martha Tonn, Kyle Neilson, Michelle Nilsson, Ken Ogorek, Dr. Claude Sasso, Scott Sollom, Deacon Jim Tighe, Mary Ann Weisinger, and Gloria Zapiain.

Augustine Institute
6160 South Syracuse Way, Suite 310
Greenwood Village, CO 80111
Information: 303-937-4420
Formed.org

Printed in the United States of America
ISBN 978-0-9972037-0-7

SYMBOLON TABLE OF CONTENTS

Session 1
THE JOURNEY OF FAITH: Trinity, Faith, & the God Who Is Love 7

Session 2
DIVINE REVELATION: God Seeking Us & the Compass for Our Lives 15

Session 3
THE BIBLE: God's Love Letter to Humanity 21

Session 4
THE STORY OF SALVATION: Creation, Fall, & Redemption 27

Session 5
WHO IS JESUS?: Just a Good Man or Lord of Our Lives? 35

Session 6
THE PASCHAL MYSTERY: The Mystery of Jesus's Death & Resurrection 43

Session 7
THE HOLY SPIRIT AND THE LIFE OF GRACE: God's Divine Life Within Us 51

Session 8
WHY DO I NEED THE CHURCH?: The Mystery of the Catholic Church 57

Session 9
MARY AND THE SAINTS: Our Spiritual Mother & the Communion of Saints 63

Session 10
THE LAST THINGS: What Happens After We Die? 69

What does *Symbolon* mean?

In the early Church, Christians described their Creed, their summary statement of faith, as the *symbolon*, the "seal" or "symbol of the faith."

In the ancient world, the Greek word *symbolon* typically described an object like a piece of parchment, a seal, or a coin that was cut in half and given to two parties. It served as a means of recognition and confirmed a relationship between the two. When the halves of the *symbolon* were reassembled, the owner's identity was verified and the relationship confirmed.

In like manner, the Creed served as a means of Christian recognition. Someone who confessed the Creed could be identified as a true Christian. Moreover, they were assured that what they professed in the Creed brought them in unity with the faith the Apostles originally proclaimed.

This series is called *Symbolon* because it intends to help bring people deeper into that communion of apostolic faith that has existed for 2,000 years in the Church that Christ founded.

AN INTRODUCTION TO SYMBOLON

Welcome to *Symbolon*! Whether you are looking to grow in your Faith or just learning about the Catholic Church for the first time, Symbolon will take you through a journey into the timeless beauty and truths of the Catholic Faith and reveal God's incredible love for us—the story of our salvation.

These ten sessions of *Symbolon—Knowing the Faith*, will take you through the Creed, or statement of beliefs that Catholics all around the world profess at every Mass. Filmed on location in Rome, the Holy Land, Calcutta, and in the Augustine Institute studios in Denver, CO, *Symbolon* is not just about an intellectual understanding of Catholicism, but a journey of faith, discovery, and friendship with Christ that will make a lasting impression on our lives. Featuring dozens of nationally known teachers, *Symbolon* unveils the beauty and richness of the Catholic story, and brings us into a personal encounter with Jesus Christ, his plan for our lives, and how we can live this plan more deeply in our daily lives.

Your Participant's Guide will be your companion on this journey of faith as you view the DVD's, participate in small group discussion, and engage in prayerful meditation on God's plan for your life.

PARTICIPATING IN A SYMBOLON SESSION

Everything you need to participate in a *Symbolon* session is provided for you. Your Participant's Guide and other resources are carefully crafted to lead you through an opening of your heart and mind to God's Word, into the key truths of the particular doctrine that is the focus of the session, and ultimately to make a response of faith by turning more fully to the Lord with each session.

Your Participant's Guide will guide you through the steps of the session and provide plenty of space for you to take notes and make reflections for later consideration.

A typical *Symbolon* session consists of:

- **Opening Prayer:** The session opens with a prayer drawn from the rich tradition of the Church and writings of the saints. You can read along during the prayer and refer back to it during the week.

- **Introduction:** Your leader will give a brief overview of the topic, including the key points for the session. This helps you see the "big picture" of the topic and its relevance for your daily life.

- **Video Part I:** The first video introduces the topic and helps establish its relevance as you seek to deepen your relationship with God and his Church.

- **Proclamation:** Your leader will give a brief summary statement of the doctrine that is the focus of the session. It is a bold statement of faith in what God has revealed and an overview of the doctrine you will be learning about in more detail in the rest of the video.

- **Video Part II:** The second video goes into more depth on the topic and gives a brief but thorough explanation of the essential truths that can unlock your understanding of the Church's teaching. It also includes a section on life application, calling you to a deeper conversion and inviting you to give your life more to Jesus through a particular aspect of the Faith.

- **Life Application:** After the video, you will have a chance to reflect on discussion questions designed to help you more deeply understand and explore the key points of the session. In addition, the "Call to Conversion" will help apply what you have learned to your daily life through prayer and reflection on key verses from Scripture, teachings, and practical personal reflection questions.

- **Closing Prayer:** Each session concludes with a prayer that reflects fundamental teachings and helps you to focus more deeply on the truths that were revealed.

In addition, your Participant's Guide contains references and resources for further reading and study. You are encouraged to memorize and reflect on a Scripture Verse of the Week that is included with every session. These bonus materials will help you nurture the grace and faith that has been poured out through your catechetical session.

Symbolon is your guide to the depth and breadth of the Catholic Faith. By bearing witness to the beauty of the teachings and the tradition of the Catholic Church, *Symbolon* enables you to grow in knowledge of the Catholic Faith and in relationship with our Lord along with others in your community. Through this comprehensive program, your life, we hope, will be transformed by God's truth and grace.

NOTES

NOTES

Session 1

THE JOURNEY OF FAITH

Session **1** THE JOURNEY OF FAITH

THE JOURNEY OF FAITH:
Trinity, Faith, & the God Who Is Love

INTRODUCTION

Welcome to the first session of *Symbolon*. This week you and your fellow participants are beginning a journey of faith that will delve into the heart of the teachings of the Catholic Church. Some of the things we cover you may already be familiar with, and others may be totally new, but today we begin with some basic fundamentals like the Creed—the statement of belief that lies at the heart of the Faith—and the Trinity, the great mystery of the one God who exists as three Persons.

May this journey we are beginning prove to be rewarding, inspiring, and most of all life-changing!

THIS SESSION WILL COVER:

- **The God who is Love—the mystery of the Holy Trinity**
- **Why God made us and the relationship he wants to have with us**
- **How faith is our response to God's invitation**
- **How to live our relationship with God: three practical tips for prayer**

Photo Credit: St. Peter's Square © Anshar/Shutterstock.com

Session 1 — THE JOURNEY OF FAITH

🔥 OPENING PRAYER

"O Lord, you have searched me
and known me.
You know when I sit down
and when I rise up;
you discern my thoughts from far away.
You search out my path
and my lying down,
and are acquainted with all my ways.
Even before a word is on my tongue,
O Lord, you know it completely.
For it was you
who formed my inward parts;
you knit me together
in my mother's womb.
I praise you, for I am fearfully and
wonderfully made." —Psalm 139:1–4, 13–14

> *"Prayer is the inner bath of love into which the soul plunges itself."*
> —St. John Vianney

❓ DISCUSSION QUESTIONS

1. Faith is our response to the God who longs to make himself known to us. How do we make that response and how is faith more than just believing in God?

2. The Holy Trinity is revealed to us through Jesus Christ. In other words, God wanted us to know, as the *Catechism* says, that "God is one but not solitary" (CCC 254).

   Why do you think God wants you to know that he is not solitary?

3. According to the video, what are three key elements of prayer?

Photo Credit: Mary praying © Bogdan Vasilescu/Shutterstock.com

Session **1** THE JOURNEY OF FAITH

CALL TO CONVERSION

After spending a few moments in prayer, write down your thoughts and reflections on the following questions:

#1 Jesus says to each of us, "Come, follow me." Envision Jesus saying that to you right now. How would you respond? What fears or hesitancies might you have about following Jesus in your life? Remember that Jesus repeatedly said, "Do not be afraid."

_____
_____
_____
_____
_____

#2 As in any relationship, a relationship with God involves conversation. What can you do this week to make more time for prayer—for talking to God—in your life? Choose a time of day that you will reserve for getting to know God better. You may want to put it as an appointment in your calendar so that you don't forget.

_____
_____
_____
_____
_____

#3 Reflect on the following quote about prayer from St. Ignatius of Loyola, the founder of the order of Jesuits.

> *"We must speak to God as a friend speaks to his friend, servant to his master; now asking some favor, now acknowledging our faults, and communicating to Him all that concerns us, our thoughts, our fears, our projects, our desires, and in all things seeking His counsel."*

What is your experience with prayer? Have you ever spoken to God as a friend? Do you feel comfortable sharing all of your thoughts, even

Photo Credit: The Calling of Matthew / Cameraphoto Arte, Venice / Art Resource, NY

Session **1** THE JOURNEY OF FAITH

your fears and desires, with God? Write down one fear and one desire that you could share with God this week.

_____
_____
_____
_____
_____
_____
_____
_____

#4 Jesus called those who came to him to believe in him, that they might have life abundant. Not everyone, however, answered the call to follow him. How will you respond?

_____
_____
_____
_____
_____
_____
_____
_____
_____
_____

Session **1** THE JOURNEY OF FAITH

CLOSING PRAYER
Psalm 23

The LORD is my shepherd,
there is nothing I lack.
In green pastures he makes me lie down;
to still waters he leads me;
he restores my soul.
He guides me along right paths
for the sake of his name.
Even though I walk through the valley of the shadow of death,
I will fear no evil, for you are with me;
your rod and your staff comfort me.
You set a table before me
in front of my enemies;
You anoint my head with oil;
my cup overflows.
Indeed, goodness and mercy will pursue me
all the days of my life;
I will dwell in the house of the LORD
for endless days.

Photo Credit: Pilgrims on the way to Emnaus / Erich Lessing / Art Resource, NY

Session 1 — THE JOURNEY OF FAITH

SCRIPTURE VERSE FOR THE WEEK

Here is a verse from the Bible that you can memorize and reflect on this week to help you apply today's session to your daily life:

 "With all of these, take the shield of faith, with which you will be able to quench all the flaming arrows of the evil one." —Ephesians 6:16

DO YOU WANT TO HAVE A MORE PERSONAL RELATIONSHIP WITH GOD?

TO ENRICH YOUR CATHOLIC FAITH, VISIT FORMED.org

Where you'll find helpful videos, audio presentations, and ebooks from the most trustworthy presenters in the Catholic world.

For Further Reading:

For more in-depth reading about the journey of faith, see the following *Catechism* passages:

- *Faith as our response to God: CCC 166*
- *Prayer: CCC 2725, 2737, 2742–2745*
- *Why God made us: CCC 294*
- *The Trinity: CCC 238–248*

If you don't have an approved Catholic translation of the Bible, such as the New American Bible or the Revised Standard Version Catholic Edition, in your home, obtain one or find one online at www.ignatius.com.

Other Resources:

- *United States Catholic Catechism for Adults*, **Chapters 1, 5, 35, 36**
- *Time for God* **by Jacques Philippe**
- *Introduction to the Devout Life* **by St. Francis de Sales**
- *Praying Scripture for a Change* **by Tim Gray**

Session **1** THE JOURNEY OF FAITH

NOTES

Session 2

DIVINE
REVELATION

Session **2** DIVINE REVELATION

DIVINE REVELATION:
God Seeking Us & the Compass for our Lives

INTRODUCTION

Today, when people think about God, they often envision an impersonal force "out there"—a God who exists, who made the universe and who may even be a good God, but not someone who interacts in this world and is personally involved in our lives. Christians, however, believe in a personal God—a God who loves us, has a plan for our lives, and wants a personal relationship with us. He loves us so much that he actually seeks us out and makes himself known to us.

THIS SESSION WILL COVER:

- **Divine Revelation: why and how God reveals himself to us**
- **Jesus as the fulfillment of God's revelation**
- **The transmission of Divine Revelation through Sacred Scripture and Sacred Tradition**
- **The Magisterium as the authoritative interpreter of Scripture and Tradition**

Cover Photo Credit, Photo Credit: Delivering the keys of the kingdom to Saint Peter / Scala / Art Resource, NY

Session 2 DIVINE REVELATION

OPENING PRAYER

Father in Heaven,
Give us the power of your grace
that we might always walk
in the way you have revealed
through your Son, Jesus Christ.
Free us from the darkness of our own desires
and bring us into the light of your truth.
Form our lives according to your will,
mold our hearts by your love.
And grant that we might always
be open and receptive
to the guidance of your Church.
We ask this in the name of the One who has
promised to be with us always,
now and forever. Amen.

"God seeks us where we are, not so that we stay there, but so that we may come to be where He is, so that we may get beyond ourselves."
—Pope Benedict XVI

DISCUSSION QUESTIONS

1. What is inconsistent with this line of reasoning: "There is a God, God is love, but we can't know with confidence who God is and what his will is for us"?

2. Why do you think the Church from earliest times chose to use the word revelation, or unveiling, to describe how God has communicated to us?

3. In the video, the presenter used the imagery of a three-legged stool to describe how Divine Revelation is handed on. What are the three "legs" of the stool?

Photo Credit: Mary praying © Bogdan Vasilescu/Shutterstock.com

CALL TO CONVERSION

After spending a few moments in prayer, write down your thoughts and reflections on the following questions:

#1 Jesus said, *"I am the way, the truth and the life. No one comes to the Father except through me"* (John 14:6). Do I really accept Jesus's revelation as the standard of truth for my life, or do I tend to make up my own moral and religious truth? Do I believe that the Gospel of Jesus Christ measures my life, or do I view myself as measuring him, picking and choosing what I want to accept from Christ's teachings, and setting aside what I don't want to follow?

_____
_____
_____
_____
_____
_____
_____

#2 What can I do this week to allow God's revelation to guide me more in my life—in my moral decisions, in my prayer, in my relationships, and in what I consider most important in life? How can I entrust my life more to Jesus and follow God's ways more?

_____
_____
_____
_____
_____
_____
_____
_____

Session 2 DIVINE REVELATION

#3 Reflect on the following quote about the teaching authority of the Catholic Church from George Weigel, biographer of Pope St. John Paul II.

"The Catholic Church believes that the truths it has been given by Christ free us as well as bind us. They are liberating truths. To accept the Church's teaching as authoritative and binding is only a 'restriction' on my freedom if I imagine freedom to be an unbridled exercise of my imagination and will. (And in that case, I have chained myself to my own willfulness.) If freedom has something to do with learning what is genuinely good, for myself and for others, then the truth about what is good for me and others isn't a restriction. It's a means of liberation" (from *The Courage to be Catholic*).

According to this quote, how can the teaching authority of the Church be a means of freedom for my life, rather than something restrictive that limits my freedom?

_____
_____
_____
_____
_____
_____

CLOSING PRAYER

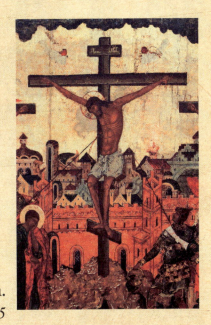

Teach me, O Lord,
the way of thy statutes;
And I will keep it to the end.
Give me understanding, that I may keep thy law
And observe it with my whole heart.
Lead me in the path of thy commandments,
For I delight in it…
How sweet are thy words to my taste,
Sweeter than honey to my mouth!
Through thy precepts I get understanding…
Thy word is a lamp to my feet and a light to my path.
—Psalm 119:33–35, 103–105

Photo Credit: Passion of Christ © Vibrant Image Studio/Shutterstock.com

Session 2 DIVINE REVELATION

SCRIPTURE VERSE FOR THE WEEK

Here is a verse from the Bible that you can memorize and reflect on this week to help you apply today's session to your daily life:

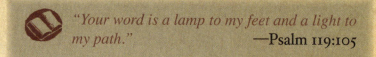

"Your word is a lamp to my feet and a light to my path." —Psalm 119:105

DO YOU WANT TO KNOW MORE ABOUT HOW GOD REVEALS HIMSELF?

TO ENRICH YOUR CATHOLIC FAITH, VISIT FORMED.org

Where you'll find helpful videos, audio presentations, and ebooks from the most trustworthy presenters in the Catholic world.

For Further Reading:

For more in-depth reading about Divine Revelation, see the following *Catechism* passages:

- *Revelation and the Plan of Salvation: CCC 50–53*
- *How God has revealed himself in the Old Testament: CCC 54–64*
- *Jesus, the fullness of Revelation: CCC 65–73*
- *How this Revelation is handed on to us: CCC 74*
- *Apostolic Tradition and Authority: CCC 75–79*
- *The Magisterium CCC 84–95*

Other Resources:

- *United States Catholic Catechism for Adults,* Chapters 2 and 3
- *The Bible Compass* by Dr. Edward Sri

For additional information on Apostolic and Authority, see the following Scripture passages:

- *Matthew 10:1–6, 10, 40*
- *Matthew 16:18–22*
- *2 Thessalonians 2:15*
- *1 Corinthians 11:23–24*
- *1 Corinthians 15:3–5*

Session 3

THE BIBLE

Session **3** THE BIBLE

THE BIBLE:
God's Love Letter to Humanity

INTRODUCTION

What do you know about the Bible? Perhaps you are coming from a faith tradition that emphasizes Scripture reading, and you know a great deal. But maybe all you know about the Bible is that it is a famous and holy book. Whatever you know (or don't know), this week's session will introduce you to the Catholic understanding of Scripture, how it fits into God's plan of salvation for our lives, and how the Catholic Church has been the guardian of the Bible since the very beginning of Christianity.

THIS SESSION WILL COVER:

- **The Bible as God's loving communication with each of us**
- **What we mean when we say the Bible is inspired by the Holy Spirit**
- **The Catholic approach to interpreting Scripture correctly**
- **How the Church discerns which books are part of the Bible (the canon of Scripture)**
- **How we can know with confidence that the Bible contains God's revelation for our lives**
- **How to start studying the Bible and praying with God's Word**

Cover Photo Credit, Photo Credit: Latin Bible © Tom Grundy/Shutterstock.com

Session 3 THE BIBLE

⚝ OPENING PRAYER

O Lord Jesus Christ,
open the eyes of my heart,
that I may hear your word
and understand and do your will,
for I am a sojourner upon the earth.
Hide not your commandments from me,
but open my eyes, that I may perceive the wonders of your law.
Speak unto me the hidden and secret things of your wisdom.
On you do I set my hope, O my God,
that you shall enlighten my mind
and understanding with the light of your knowledge,
not only to cherish those things
which are written, but to do them;
that in reading the lives and sayings of the saints
I may not sin,
but that such may serve for my restoration, enlightenment
and sanctification, for the salvation of my soul,
and the inheritance of life everlasting.
For you are the enlightenment of those
who lie in darkness,
and from you comes every good deed
and every gift. Amen.
　　　—St. John Chrysostom

> *"If you believe what you like in the gospels, and reject what you don't like, it is not the gospel you believe, but yourself."*
> —St. Augustine

❓ DISCUSSION QUESTIONS

1. Why is it true that "ignorance of Scripture is ignorance of Christ"?

2. According to the video, what does it mean that Catholics don't interpret the Bible in a literalistic way, but they do read the Bible literarily? What examples does the presenter give?

3. Let's say a friend of yours, while speaking about a passage she was reading in the Bible, states, "It was like God was speaking directly to me—directly into a situation in my life—when I read the passage." How is this possible?

CALL TO CONVERSION

After spending a few moments in prayer, write down your thoughts and reflections on the following questions:

#1 Psalm 119:105 says, "Your word is a lamp to my feet, a light for my path." What does this passage mean to me? Am I willing to read God's Word in Scripture with an open heart and mind, expecting that God will give me insights for my life?

_____
_____
_____
_____
_____
_____
_____

> *"As Paul says, Christ is the power of God and the wisdom of God, and if the man who does not know Scripture does not know the power and wisdom of God, then ignorance of Scripture is ignorance of Christ."* —St. Jerome

#2 What can I do this week to make the reading of Scripture a greater part of my life? (Consider reading the Bible, perhaps starting with the Gospel of Luke as suggested in the video.)

_____
_____
_____
_____
_____
_____
_____
_____
_____

Photo Credit: St. John the Evangelist / National Trust Photo Library / Art Resource, NY

#3 Reflect on the following quote from Pope St. Gregory:

"The Holy Bible is like a mirror before our mind's eye. In it we see our inner face. From the Scriptures we can learn our spiritual deformities and beauties. And there too we discover the progress we are making and how far we are from perfection."

How might thinking of the Bible as a mirror and as a way to learn about my spiritual progress make a difference in how I listen to the readings at Mass? What can I do to be better prepared for the Scripture readings each week?

_____
_____
_____
_____
_____

CLOSING PRAYER

Prayer Before Reading Scripture

We praise and thank you glorious Lord Jesus Christ, for being present among us and in us.
In us you praise the Father with the voice of the Spirit, whom you have given us.
Lord, may this voice of the Spirit be roused in us as we listen to the words of Scripture in a manner that is worthy and fitting, appropriate to the meaning of the text and in harmony with what is revealed to us. Make us ready to recognize how we can correspond to the teaching and example proposed to us, for you are God, living and reigning for ever and ever. Amen.

—Carlo Maria Martini, SJ

Photo Credit: Christ appearing to his disciples at the Mount of Olives / Scala / Art Resource, NY

Session 3 THE BIBLE

SCRIPTURE VERSE FOR THE WEEK

Here is a verse from the Bible that you can memorize and reflect on this week to help you apply today's session to your daily life:

> *"For the word of God is living and active, sharper than any two-edged sword, piercing to the division of soul and spirit, of joints and marrow, and discerning the thoughts and intentions of the heart."* —Hebrews 4:12

DO YOU WANT TO KNOW MORE ABOUT THE BIBLE?

TO ENRICH YOUR CATHOLIC FAITH, VISIT FORMED.org

Where you'll find helpful videos, audio presentations, and ebooks from the most trustworthy presenters in the Catholic world.

For Further Reading:

For more in-depth reading about the Sacred Scripture, see the following *Catechism* passages:

- *Christ as the Word of God: CCC 101–104*
- *Inspiration and the truth of Scripture: CCC 105–108*
- *The Holy Spirit and Sacred Scripture: CCC 109–119*
- *Books of the Old Testament: CCC 120–123*
- *The New Testament canon: CCC 124–127*
- *Scripture and the Church: CCC 131–133*

Other Resources:

- *United States Catholic Catechism for Adults*, **Chapter 3**
- *A Father Who Keeps His Promises: God's Covenant Love in Scripture* **by Scott Hahn**
- *Walking with God: A Journey through the Bible* **by Tim Gray and Jeff Cavins**
- *Catholic Bible Dictionary* **by Scott Hahn**
- *Where is THAT in the Bible?* **by Patrick Madrid**
- *The Bible Compass: A Catholic's Guide to Navigating the Scriptures* **by Dr. Edward Sri**
- *The Ignatius Catholic Study Bible series* **by Scott Hahn and Curtis Mitch**

Session 4

THE STORY OF SALVATION

Session **4** THE STORY OF SALVATION

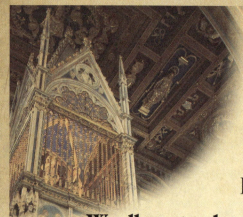

THE STORY OF SALVATION:
Creation, Fall, & Redemption

INTRODUCTION

We all want to know that our lives have meaning. But the modern world tries to tell us that we are simply insignificant specks in the universe, and that there is no real meaning to life. Our choices don't matter. How we live our lives doesn't matter. Each individual should just do whatever he or she pleases.

Nothing could be further from the truth. Our lives are a part of a much larger story. We are God's beloved children, created in his own image, and made for greatness. Despite the fact that we live in a fallen world, God, who is all-powerful and all-loving, reaches out to us, desiring to bring us back into unity with him and inviting us to help bring his goodness and his love into a broken world that has turned away from him.

This story of salvation, which we recall through the words of the Creed, reminds us that there is a reason for our existence. Because each of us is loved by God, each of us has a role to play in God's creation and his great story of love, a role that only we can play. When we refuse God's loving invitation, all of creation is the poorer.

THIS SESSION WILL COVER:

- **The three major parts in the story of salvation: Creation, Fall, and Redemption**
- **How originally we were united with God and experienced harmony within the human family**
- **How sin broke our unity and left us with an inclination toward sin, called concupiscence**
- **How Jesus came to restore us to the Father, but also to establish the Catholic Church to gather the broken family of humanity into the united family of God**

Session 4 THE STORY OF SALVATION

OPENING PRAYER

We pray to you, O Lord,
who are the supreme Truth,
and all truth is from you.
We beseech you, O Lord,
who are the highest Wisdom,
and all the wise depend on you for their wisdom.
You are the supreme Joy,
and all who are happy
owe it to you.
You are the Light of minds,
and all receive their understanding from you.
We love, we love you above all.
We seek you, we follow you,
and we are ready to serve you.
We desire to dwell under your power
for you are the King of all. Amen.
—St. Albert the Great, one of the great teachers or Doctors of the Church

> *"O happy fault, O necessary sin of Adam, which gained for us so great a Redeemer!"* (From the Exsultet or Easter Proclamation)

DISCUSSION QUESTIONS

1. Dr. Sri talks about the story of salvation and how this story plays a role in each of our lives. What does it mean that "our modern world has lost its story," and why does that matter?

2. Dr. Sri speaks of a timeline that demonstrates how salvation history is the growth of God's family as he draws mankind back to himself. Here is the process by which God's family grows:

   One Couple→ One Family→ One Tribe→ One Nation→ One Kingdom→ One Church
   (Adam & Eve)→ (Noah)→ (Abraham)→ (Moses)→ (David)→ (Jesus and the Apostles)

Session 4 THE STORY OF SALVATION

Consistent throughout salvation history are covenants. How does entering into a covenant "define the relationship" between God and his people?

3. In the video, we were reminded that we all have an inclination toward sin. As St. Paul says in Romans 7:15, "For I do not do what I want, but I do what I hate." Recall sometime in the last week when you didn't do something that you knew you should or did something that you knew you shouldn't. Ask God to help you make a better choice the next time a similar circumstance arises.

CALL TO CONVERSION

After spending a few moments in prayer, write down your thoughts and reflections on the following questions:

#1 Now is your time to enter the story of salvation. What might you be putting off with regard to your faith? Is God asking you to do something right now? If you have been reluctant or afraid to commit your life to Jesus, spend some time writing about the reasons why. Are you afraid of what your friends or members of your family might say? Pray with the father who asked Jesus to cure his son: "Lord, I believe. Help my disbelief!"

_____
_____
_____
_____

Photo Credit: Scala / Art Resource, NY

Session **4** THE STORY OF SALVATION

#2 Read the following quote from Pope Benedict XVI:

"Each of us is the result of a thought of God. Each of us is willed. Each of us is loved. Each of us is necessary."

List two or three roles that you play in your life, such as parent, worker, or friend. Now consider what would happen if you didn't live those relationships well. Who would suffer? What wouldn't be accomplished? Say a prayer of gratitude that you have been, in the words of Psalm 139:14, "fearfully and wonderfully made" and ask God for the grace to help you fulfill your responsibilities with the people and missions he has entrusted to you.

_____
_____
_____
_____

#3 In his "Meditation on Two Standards," St. Ignatius of Loyola, the founder of the Jesuits, challenges us to see the real struggle between good and evil in the world today. Following the spirit of his meditation, prayerfully imagine a battlefield with Jesus, the commander-in-chief of good, on one side calling all people under his standard (his flag). He calls men and women to follow him with humility, patience, generosity, purity, poverty, and sacrificial love. Next, imagine on the other side of the field Satan, the chief enemy of all that is good, inviting people under his flag. He entices people away from Jesus through the lure of riches, the pursuit of worldly honor and success, pride, and lust, and he distracts them from the true meaning of life with constant busyness and amusements. Finally, put yourself on that field and honestly consider: Which side attracts you the most? In what ways are you pursuing the standard of Christ? In what ways do you find yourself lured by the standard of the devil? In what ways can you live more for Christ's kingdom and not Satan's?

_____
_____
_____
_____

CLOSING PRAYER

We give you praise,
Father most holy,
for you are great
and you have fashioned all your works
in wisdom and in love.
You formed man in your own image
and entrusted the whole world to his care,
so that in serving you alone, the Creator,
he might have dominion over all creatures.
And when through disobedience
he had lost your friendship,
you did not abandon him
to the domain of death...
And you so loved the world,
Father most holy
that in the fullness of time
you sent your Only Begotten Son
to be our Savior...
To accomplish your plan,
he gave himself up to death, and,
rising from the dead,
he destroyed death and restored life.
And that we might live no longer for ourselves
but for him who died and rose again for us,
he sent the Holy Spirit from you, Father,
as the first fruits for those who believe,
so that, bringing to perfection his work in the world,
he might sanctify creation to the full.

—From the *Roman Missal*, Eucharistic Prayer IV

Session 4 THE STORY OF SALVATION

SCRIPTURE VERSE FOR THE WEEK

Here is a verse from the Bible that you can memorize and reflect on this week to help you apply today's session to your daily life:

 "For God so loved the world that he gave his only Son, so that everyone who believes in him might not perish but might have eternal life." —John 3:16

DO YOU WANT TO UNDERSTAND THE "BIG PICTURE" OF THE CATHOLIC FAITH?

TO ENRICH YOUR CATHOLIC FAITH, VISIT FORMED.org

Where you'll find helpful videos, audio presentations, and ebooks from the most trustworthy presenters in the Catholic world.

For Further Reading:

For more in-depth reading about the story of salvation, see the following *Catechism* passages:

- *Created in the image of God: CCC 356–358*
- *Before the Fall: CCC 376–379*
- *Original Sin: CCC 396–405*
- *The gift of Jesus: CCC 457–460*
- *The Catholic Church: CCC 830–848*
- *Sending of the Holy Spirit: CCC 731–737*
- *The Last Judgment: CCC 1038–1041*

Other Resources:

- *United States Catholic Catechism for Adults,* **Chapters 6–10**
- *Catholicism: A Journey to the Heart of Faith* **by Fr. Robert Barron**

Session 4 THE STORY OF SALVATION

NOTES

Session 5

WHO IS JESUS?

WHO IS JESUS?
Just a Good Man or Lord of our Lives?

INTRODUCTION

Who is Jesus?

People have been asking that question for 2,000 years. Today most would agree that Jesus was a historical figure, a first-century Jew who was crucified by the Romans in the city of Jerusalem. Many would even agree that he offered some good moral teachings. However, the idea that Jesus could actually be God is as controversial now as it was in his own time.

However, that is exactly what Christians profess in the Creed—"I believe in one Lord Jesus Christ, the Only Begotten Son of God, born of the Father before all ages. God from God, Light from Light, true God from true God, begotten, not made, consubstantial with the Father."

For Christians, the answer to the question of Jesus's identity is simple: he is God, come to live with us.

THIS SESSION WILL COVER:

- How, in the fullness of time, God has spoken to us through his Son, Jesus
- How Jesus, the second Person of the Trinity, took on human nature without losing his divine nature
- That Jesus is the one and only mediator between God and man
- That Jesus is one divine Person who possesses two natures
- Why Jesus became man so that we can be reconciled to God and know God's love

Cover Photo Credit, Photo Credit: Byzantine Mosaic © Stefan Holm/Shutterstock.com

Session 5 WHO IS JESUS?

OPENING PRAYER

O my Divine Savior,
Transform me into yourself.
May my hands be the hands of Jesus.
Grant that every faculty of my body
May serve only to glorify you.
Above all,
Transform my soul and all its powers
So that my memory, will, and affection
May be the memory, will, and affections
Of Jesus.
I pray you To destroy in me
All that is not of you.
Grant that I may live
But in you, by you and for you,
So that I may truly say, with St. Paul,
'I live—now not I—
But Christ lives in me.'
Amen.

—St. John Gabriel Perboyre, a French priest who died as a martyr in China on September 11, 1840

"It is Jesus that you seek when you dream of happiness; He is waiting for you when nothing else you find satisfies you; He is the beauty to which you are so attracted; it is He who provoked you with that thirst for fullness that will not let you settle for compromise; it is He who urges you to shed the masks of a false life; it is He who reads in your heart your most genuine choices, the choices that others try to stifle."
—Pope St. John Paul II, August 19, 2000 at World Youth Day in Rome
www.calledbychrist.com/mn-vocations/E-News-2011-05-Blessed-John-Paul-II-Champion-of-Catholic-Youth-and-Vocations.pdf

Photo Credit: The Good Shepherd / Gianni Dagli Orti / The Art Archive at Art Resource, NY

❓ DISCUSSION QUESTIONS

1. According to the video, what are three things Jesus did during his public ministry that point to his being truly God?

2. What do you think it means for Jesus, the divine Son of God, to be truly and fully human? Can you imagine Jesus being tired, hungry, or angry? How does seeing Jesus as having all the same feelings and experiences you have (except for sin) change the way you tell him your needs and desires in prayer?

3. Dr. Sri explained to us the meaning of the painting of Jesus in the Basilica of Saints Cosmas and Damian in Rome. How does that painting confront us with a decision we all have to make?

Photo Credit: The Last Suppe © Shutterstock.com

Session **5** WHO IS JESUS?

CALL TO CONVERSION

After spending a few moments in prayer, write down your thoughts and reflections on the following questions:

#1 Prayerfully read the following quote from C.S. Lewis's *Mere Christianity*, which was mentioned in the video.

"I am trying here to prevent anyone saying the really foolish thing that people often say about Him: I'm ready to accept Jesus as a great moral teacher, but I don't accept his claim to be God. That is the one thing we must not say. A man who was merely a man and said the sort of things Jesus said would not be a great moral teacher. He would either be a lunatic—on the level with the man who says he is a poached egg—or else he would be the Devil of Hell. You must make your choice. Either this man was, and is, the Son of God, or else a madman or something worse. You can shut him up for a fool, you can spit at him and kill him as a demon or you can fall at his feet and call him Lord and God, but let us not come with any patronizing nonsense about his being a great human teacher. He has not left that open to us. He did not intend to."
(C.S. Lewis was an Oxford professor and a famous 20th century defender of the Christian Faith. He is also the author of *The Chronicles of Narnia*.)

Now, prayerfully imagine Jesus standing before you and asking you the question he asked his Apostles: "Who do you say that I am?" How would you answer him?

_____
_____
_____
_____
_____
_____

Session 5 WHO IS JESUS?

#2 Jesus tells us to "seek first his kingdom and his righteousness" (Matthew 6:33). What do you seek first in your life? Do you truly put Jesus first in your life? Or do you seek other things to fulfill you, and have God as just a part of your life?

___

#3 Allowing Jesus to reign over our lives as Lord requires submitting our will to his. It means following his teachings, living the way he wants us to live, and trusting that he knows and desires what is best for us. Write down one or two areas in your life where the way you are living now could be more in line with Jesus's teachings. What can you do this week to begin living more with Jesus as Lord of your life?

___

 **WHO IS JESUS?**

CLOSING PRAYER

Take, O Lord,
and receive my entire liberty,
my memory,
my understanding and my whole will.
All that I am and all that I possess
you have given me:
I surrender it all to you
to be disposed of according to your will.
Give me only your love and your grace;
with these I will be rich enough,
and will desire nothing more. Amen.
—St. Ignatius of Loyola, founder of the Jesuits

SCRIPTURE VERSE FOR THE WEEK

Here is a verse from the Bible that you can memorize and reflect on this week to help you apply today's session to your daily life:

 "Jesus said to him, 'I am the way, and the truth, and the life, no one comes to the Father except but by me.'" —John 14:6

Session 5 WHO IS JESUS?

DO YOU WANT JESUS TO BE THE LORD OF YOUR LIFE?

TO ENRICH YOUR CATHOLIC FAITH, VISIT FORMED.org

Where you'll find helpful videos, audio presentations, and ebooks from the most trustworthy presenters in the Catholic world.

For Further Reading:

For more in-depth reading about the Jesus, see the following *Catechism* passages:

- *Jesus Christ: "Mediator and fullness of all revelation"*: CCC 65–67
- *True God and true man*: CCC 464–469, 479–483
- *Jesus reconciles us with God*: CCC 457–460
- *The two natures of Jesus*: CCC 470–478

Other Resources:

- *United States Catholic Catechism for Adults,* **Chapter 7**
- *Jesus of Nazareth* **(three volumes) by Pope Benedict XVI**
- *Mere Christianity* **by C.S. Lewis**
- *The Life of Christ* **by Venerable Fulton Sheen**
- *To Know Jesus Christ* **by Frank Sheed**
- *Made for More* **by Curtis Martin**

NOTES

Session 6

THE PASCHAL MYSTERY

Session **6** THE PASCHAL MYSTERY

THE PASCHAL MYSTERY:
The Mystery of Jesus's Death & Resurrection

INTRODUCTION

Some of us might be so accustomed to seeing images of crosses in our churches, we may not realize that in the ancient world, the cross was a horrifying image. For people living 2,000 years ago, wearing a cross like jewelry around one's neck would be as shocking as wearing a little electric chair around our necks would be today. The cross was a well-known means of capital punishment, just as an electric chair has been in modern times. And yet the cross is the primary symbol of our Faith because it is through Jesus's Death on the Cross that we have been given the gift of salvation and eternal life.

We call Jesus's work of redemption, accomplished principally through his Passion, Death, Resurrection, and Ascension into Heaven—the Paschal Mystery. The word *Paschal* refers to Jesus's offering of his life as the new Passover (or Paschal) lamb for our salvation.

THIS SESSION WILL COVER:

- **How the Cross "works"—how it brings about our salvation**
- **How Christ, being fully human and fully divine, was able to heal our relationship with God through his sacrificial Death**
- **The meaning of Jesus going to the realm of the dead and opening Heaven's gates**
- **That by his Death, Jesus liberates us from sin**
- **That by his Resurrection, he opens us to new life**
- **How Jesus invites us to unite our entire lives with his self-giving love on the Cross**

Cover Photo Credit, Photo Credit: Passion of Christ © Vibrant Image Studio/Shutterstock.com

Session **6** THE PASCHAL MYSTERY

OPENING PRAYER

Hail, sweet Jesus!
Praise, honor, and glory be to you, O Christ,
who of your own accord did embrace death,
and, recommending yourself to your heavenly Father,
bowing down your venerable head, did yield up your spirit.
Truly thus giving up your life for your sheep,
you have shown yourself to be a good shepherd.
You did die, O only-begotten Son of God.
You did die, O my beloved Savior, that I might live forever.
O how great hope,
how great confidence have I reposed in your death and your Blood!
I glorify and praise your Holy Name,
acknowledging my infinite obligations to you.
O good Jesus,
by your bitter death and Passion,
give me grace and pardon.
Give unto the faithful departed rest and life everlasting.
Amen.
—Dom Augustine Baker, 1575–1641

> *"We adore you, O Christ, and we praise you because, by your holy cross, you have redeemed the world."*
> —From St. Alphonsus Liguori's Stations of the Cross, a devotion meditating on Jesus's carrying the Cross and his Death on Calvary

DISCUSSION QUESTIONS

1. Scripture tells us that the Son of God humbled himself to become man, and was obedient to the Father even to his Death on the Cross (Philippians 2:5-11). What does God's willingness to enter our world, embrace our humanity, and die for our sins tell us about God's love for us? How can Jesus's self-sacrificial love be an example for our lives?

2. Generally people try to avoid suffering. In the news we might even hear about some people with terminal illnesses who have committed suicide in order to avoid their suffering. But let's consider for a moment this quote from John 12:24: "Unless a grain of wheat falls into the earth

and dies, it remains just a single grain; but if it dies, it bears much fruit." Here's another way of saying that: "Every death presents an opportunity for a resurrection. Every suffering can be a tremendous gift." How can suffering or carrying a cross be a great gift?

3. Dr. Sri says that there are two ways to live your life: the way of self and the way of the Cross. Why is there more joy and fulfillment found in the way of the Cross?

CALL TO CONVERSION

After spending a few moments in prayer, write down your thoughts and reflections on the following questions:

#1 Have you ever considered what it means that Jesus died for you and paid the price for your sins? Take a few minutes now to thank him for the great gift that he gave you. You may want to silently pray the following prayer called the Act of Contrition, which expresses heartfelt sorrow for our sins:

> *"My God, I am sorry for my sins with all my heart. In choosing to do wrong and failing to do good, I have sinned against you whom I should love above all things. I firmly intend, with your help, to do penance, to sin no more, and to avoid whatever leads me to sin. Our Savior Jesus Christ suffered and died for us. In His name, my God, have mercy. Amen."*

_____
_____
_____
_____
_____

Photo Credit: The Crucifixion / Scala / Art Resource, NY

#2 In the video, we heard that because we live in a broken world, we should never ask, "Will I suffer?" but rather "What will I do when I suffer?" As St. Peter says, "Beloved, do not be surprised at the fiery trial when it comes upon you to test you, as though something strange were happening to you" (1 Peter 4:12). In fact, Jesus himself entered our humanity and has shared in our suffering. And he wants to be with us to help us in the midst of our trials. What do you do when you encounter suffering in your life? Do you turn to God or do you turn away from God? Make a commitment now to turn to God for help the next time suffering enters your life.

_____
_____
_____
_____
_____

#3 Reflect on the following quote:

"Whoever wants to be my disciple must deny themselves and take up their cross daily and follow me." —Luke 9:23

Consider some ways you can imitate Christ's sacrificial love more in your life. For example, how can you be more generous in your relationship with God? What are some ways you can deny yourself—your time, comfort, or desires—and make sacrifices to serve better the people God has placed in your life?

_____
_____
_____
_____
_____

Session **6** THE PASCHAL MYSTERY

CLOSING PRAYER

O Jesus, you have called me to suffer
because you on your part suffered for me,
leaving me an example that I might follow.
When you were insulted,
you did not return the insult.
When you were mistreated,
you did not counter with threats
but entrusted yourself to the One who judges justly.
By your wounds we are healed.
Help me to imitate you in suffering.
Let me break with sin by means of my sufferings,
so that I may no longer live
according to the lusts of sinners
but according to the will of the Father.
Since you yourself have suffered and been tempted,
I know that you are able to bring aid to all
who suffer and are tempted.
I entrust myself to you and to the Father, my Creator,
knowing that you will never fail me.
Amen.

—Prayer to Imitate the Suffering Christ

http://www.2heartsnetwork.org/wounds.htm

Here is a verse from the Bible that you can memorize and reflect on this week to help you apply today's session to your daily life:

 "I have been crucified with Christ and I no longer live, but Christ lives in me. The life I now live in the body, I live by faith in the Son of God, who loved me and gave himself for me." —Galatians 2:20

Photo Credit: The Crucifixion / Scala / Art Resource, NY

Session **6** THE PASCHAL MYSTERY

DO YOU WANT TO UNITE YOUR LIFE MORE WITH JESUS'S DEATH AND RESURRECTION?

TO ENRICH YOUR CATHOLIC FAITH, VISIT FORMED.org

Where you'll find helpful videos, audio presentations, and ebooks from the most trustworthy presenters in the Catholic world.

For Further Reading:

For more in-depth reading about the Paschal Mystery, see the following *Catechism* passages:

- *The Trinity: CCC 238-248, 452-455*
- *Value of Christ's sacrifice: CCC 616–617*
- *The descent into Hell: CCC 632–635*
- *The meaning of the Resurrection: CCC 651–655*
- *Jesus precedes us into Heaven: CCC 665-667*
- *Our participation in Christ's sacrifice: CCC 618*

Other Resources:

- *United States Catholic Catechism for Adults,* **Chapter 8**
- *Making Sense Out of Suffering* **by Peter Kreeft**
- *Jesus of Nazareth: Holy Week* **by Pope Benedict XVI**

Session 6 THE PASCHAL MYSTERY

NOTES

Session 7

THE HOLY SPIRIT AND THE LIFE OF GRACE

Session **7** THE HOLY SPIRIT

THE HOLY SPIRIT AND THE LIFE OF GRACE:
God's Divine Life Within Us

INTRODUCTION

A little boy in a best-selling book who is said to have died and gone to Heaven was asked to describe the Holy Spirit. He paused for a moment and then said, "Hmm, that's kind of a hard one." I think we can all identify. Describing the Holy Spirit is hard. We all have mental images of Jesus and God the Father, but the Holy Spirit...?

Perhaps you picture a dove, or tongues of fire, or a rushing wind as at the first Pentecost. Alternatively, maybe you don't have any mental picture at all. That's okay. What's more important than an image is your relationship with the Holy Spirit. It is the Holy Spirit, the third Person of the Holy Trinity—the bond of love between the Father and the Son—who comes into our souls at Baptism, making us sons and daughters of the Living God. By learning to know and love the Holy Spirit, we become transformed and we can, in the words of the traditional prayer to the Holy Spirit, help "renew the face of the earth."

THIS SESSION WILL COVER:

- How the Holy Spirit builds, animates, and sanctifies the Church, bringing souls into communion with God so that they bear fruit and give witness to Christ

- How the Holy Spirit is the bond of love between the Father and the Son, and how God's love has been poured into our hearts through the Holy Spirit

- The gifts and fruits of the Holy Spirit

- The ways the Holy Spirit sanctifies, or makes us holy

- How we are saved, and the relationship between faith and works in this process of sanctification

Cover Photo Credit, Photo Credit: St. Peter in Vatican © Dan Costa/Shutterstock.com

Session 7 THE HOLY SPIRIT

🔥 OPENING PRAYER

Come Holy Spirit,
fill the hearts of your faithful
and kindle in them the fire of your love.
Send forth your Spirit
and they shall be created.
And You shall renew the face of the earth.
O, God, who by the light of the Holy Spirit,
did instruct the hearts of the faithful,
grant that by the same Holy Spirit
we may be truly wise
and ever enjoy his consolations.
Through Christ Our Lord,
Amen.

> *"O Holy Spirit, descend plentifully into my heart. Enlighten the dark corners of this neglected dwelling and scatter there Thy cheerful beams."*
> —St. Augustine

❓ DISCUSSION QUESTIONS

1. The Holy Spirit makes sanctification possible. We know that we cannot get to Heaven on our own—we need help to get there. Justification is a very important concept to understand. What did justification, through an indwelling of the Holy Spirit, do for us?

2. How do we grow in our relationship with the Holy Spirit in our daily lives??

Photo Credit: The Calling of Matthew / National Trust Photo Library / Art Resource, NY

3. Let's say your friend says to you, "All you need to do is accept Jesus Christ as your Lord and Savior to be saved. He did all the work for us." How would you respond?

CALL TO CONVERSION

At the end of the video, we were asked two essential questions:

#1 At the end of the video, we were asked two essential questions: Will you develop a relationship with the Holy Spirit? Will you take time to ask the Spirit to guide and shape your daily life? Reflect now on your response.

_____
_____
_____
_____
_____
_____

#2 The fruits of the Holy Spirit include love, joy, peace, patience, kindness, generosity, faithfulness, and self-control. If you could choose one of these to be made manifest more in your life now, which one would you chose? Which one seems the easiest? Which one seems the hardest? Pray now that the Spirit will enter into your life and transform you with his fruits.

_____
_____
_____
_____
_____
_____

Session **7** THE HOLY SPIRIT

CLOSING PRAYER

"Come Holy Ghost, Creator Blest,
And in our hearts take up Thy rest;
Come with Thy grace and heav'nly aid
To fill the hearts which Thou hast made,
To fill the hearts which Thou hast made.
O Comfort Blest to Thee we cry,
Thou heav'nly Gift of God most high;
Thou fount of life and fire of love,
And sweet anointing from above,
And sweet anointing from above.
Praise be to Thee Father and Son,
And Holy Spirit Three in one;
And may the Son on us bestow
The gifts that from the Spirit flow,
The gifts that from the Spirit flow."
—Words: Latin, tenth century; trans. Edward Caswall, 1849,
Richard Mant, 1837, and Robert Campbell, 1850.

SCRIPTURE VERSE FOR THE WEEK

Here is a verse from the Bible that you can memorize and reflect on this week to help you apply today's session to your daily life:

 "Likewise the Spirit helps us in our weakness; for we do not know how to pray as we ought, but the Spirit himself intercedes for us with sighs too deep for words." —Romans 8:26

Photo Credit: St. Peter in Vatican © Dan Costa/Shutterstock.com

Session **7** THE HOLY SPIRIT

DO YOU WANT TO HAVE A MORE PERSONAL RELATIONSHIP WITH THE HOLY SPIRIT?

TO ENRICH YOUR CATHOLIC FAITH, VISIT FORMED.org

Where you'll find helpful videos, audio presentations, and ebooks from the most trustworthy presenters in the Catholic world.

For Further Reading:

For more in-depth reading about the Holy Spirit, see the following *Catechism* passages:

- *The Name of the Spirit: CCC 691*
- *Symbols of the Spirit: CCC 694–701*
- *The Holy Spirit as God's Gift: CCC 733–736*
- *The Spirit and the Church: CCC 737–741*
- *Justification and sanctification: CCC 1996–2000*

Other Resources:

- *United States Catholic Catechism for Adults,* **Chapters 5, 9**
- **Encyclical Letter** *Dominum et Vivificantem "Lord and Giver of Life" on the Holy Spirit* **by John Paul II**
- *The Holy Spirit* **(www.ewtn.com/faith/teachings/spirmenu.htm)**
- *Justification in Catholic Teaching* **by James Akin (www.ewtn.com/library/answers/justif.htm)**

Session 8

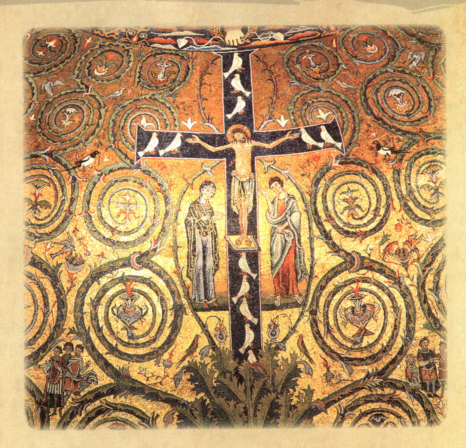

WHY DO I NEED THE CHURCH?

Session **8** WHY DO I NEED THE CHURCH?

WHY DO I NEED THE CHURCH?
The Mystery of the Catholic Church

INTRODUCTION

Have you ever heard people say they were "spiritual but not religious"? It can be hard to tell what they mean. They may mean they believe in God or a "higher power" but don't attend church. Or they might mean they don't want to have to obey any so-called "man-made" rules or regulations.

As sincere as these people may be (and many are very sincere), religion and spirituality are intricately interwoven. Jesus never expected us to follow a spiritual path without a community, the Church. The truly spiritual life is, as Jesus himself said, like a vine in which he is the trunk and we are the branches. He intends us to be united in his Church through our beliefs, our worship, and the Apostles and their successors whom he left on earth to guide us. And once we begin to understand the mystery of the Church, we realize that it is as impossible to be spiritual without being religious as it is to swim without getting into the water.

THIS SESSION WILL COVER:

- **The mystery of the Church and what it means in our lives**
- **How the Church has two dimensions: human and divine**
- **The three ways the unity of the Church is made manifest**
- **The four marks (or chief characteristics) of the Church**
- **Why Jesus established only one Church**
- **How the Church can be holy when it is filled with sinners**
- **What it means when we say the Church is apostolic**
- **Why we call the Church "Catholic"**

Cover Photo Credit, Photo Credit: San Clemente Church © VladG/Shutterstock.com

Session 8 WHY DO I NEED THE CHURCH?

🕯 OPENING PRAYER

We praise you,
O almighty and eternal God!
Who through Jesus Christ
hast revealed your glory to all nations,
to preserve the works of your mercy,
that your Church,
being spread through
the whole world,
may continue with unchanging faith
in the confession of your name.
Amen.

—www.catholic.org

"…God has saved a people. There is no full identity without belonging to a people. No one is saved alone, as an isolated individual, but God attracts us looking at the complex web of relationships that take place in the human community. God enters into this dynamic, this participation in the web of human relationships."
—Pope Francis

❓ DISCUSSION QUESTIONS

1. The Church is unique among all institutions in the world, because she has both divine and human dimensions that come together in perfect unity. What are the three ways this unity of the Church is made manifest?

2. The Church has four characteristics or distinctive marks that sets her apart from all other Christian denominations. What are these "marks of the Church" and what do they mean?

3. Let's say that your friend says to you that he (or she) is "spiritual" but not a "religious" person. What is the problem with that statement?

Photo Credit: Last Judgment / The Art Archive at Art Resource, NY

Session 8 — WHY DO I NEED THE CHURCH?

CALL TO CONVERSION

#1 In the video, we heard that Jesus wants to have a personal relationship with us in his Church, but not a private, individualistic relationship. What are the differences between a personal relationship with God in his Church and an individualistic relationship with God?

_____
_____
_____
_____
_____
_____
_____

#2 Reflect on the following quote:

> "I am the vine; you are the branches. If you remain in me and I in you, you will bear much fruit; apart from me you can do nothing. If you do not remain in me, you are like a branch that is thrown away and withers; such branches are picked up, thrown into the fire and burned. If you remain in me and my words remain in you, ask whatever you wish, and it will be done for you." —John 15:5–7

Jesus describes himself as the vine and we, united to him in the Church, are the branches. In what ways can you "remain" in Jesus? What comes to mind when you read Jesus's promise that if we remain in him, we will bear much fruit? What kind of fruit would you like to bear in this life?

_____
_____
_____
_____
_____
_____
_____
_____
_____

Session 8 WHY DO I NEED THE CHURCH?

#3 Even though most Americans claim to believe in God, more and more embrace the idea of being "spiritual" but not belonging to an organized religion or church. One of the fundamental reasons for this attitude, according to the presenters in the video, is that we don't like the idea that there is something outside of ourselves with an objective standard that has the right to guide, inform, and correct our beliefs and behavior. Some people might want the benefits of being "spiritual," but they don't want the challenges that come with real growth and transformation. Are there ways that you keep the Church and her teachings at a distance because you don't want to be challenged or have to change your life? What would you have to change or give up to fully embrace all the teachings of the Church? How might your life be different if you gave yourself over completely to Christ and his Church?

_____
_____
_____
_____
_____

CLOSING PRAYER

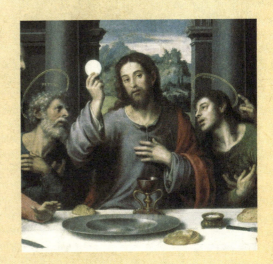

Lord Jesus Christ,
at your Last Supper
you prayed to the Father
that all should be one.
Send your Holy Spirit
upon all who bear your name
and seek to serve you.
Strengthen our faith in you,
and lead us to love one another
in humility.
May we who have been reborn
in one Baptism
be united in one faith under one Shepherd.
Amen.
—www.prayer-and-prayers.info/catholic-prayers/prayer-for-christian-unity.htm

Photo Credit: The Last Supper © shutterstock.com

Session 8 WHY DO I NEED THE CHURCH?

SCRIPTURE VERSE FOR THE WEEK

Here is a verse from the Bible that you can memorize and reflect on this week to help you apply today's session to your daily life:

"I am the vine, you are the branches. He who abides in me, and I in him, he it is that bears much fruit, for apart from me you can do nothing." —John 15:5

DO YOU REALLY NEED THE CHURCH?

TO ENRICH YOUR CATHOLIC FAITH, VISIT FORMED.org

Where you'll find helpful videos, audio presentations, and ebooks from the most trustworthy presenters in the Catholic world.

For Further Reading:

For more in-depth reading about the Church, see the following *Catechism* passages:

- *The Church is One: CCC 813–814*
- *The Church is Holy: CCC 823–825*
- *The Church is Catholic: CCC 830–831*
- *The Church is Apostolic: CCC 857*
- *The bonds of unity in the Church: CCC 815*
- *Bishops as successors of the Apostles: CCC 861–862*

Other Resources:

- *United States Catholic Catechism for Adults,* **Chapters 10, 11**
- *Called to Communion: Understanding the Church Today* **by Joseph Cardinal Ratzinger**
- *The Compact History of the Catholic Church* **by Alan Schreck Ph.D.**
- *Our Sunday Visitor's Encyclopedia of Catholic History* **by Matthew Bunson**
- *By What Authority? An Evangelical Discovers Catholic Tradition* **by Mark P. Shea**

Session 9

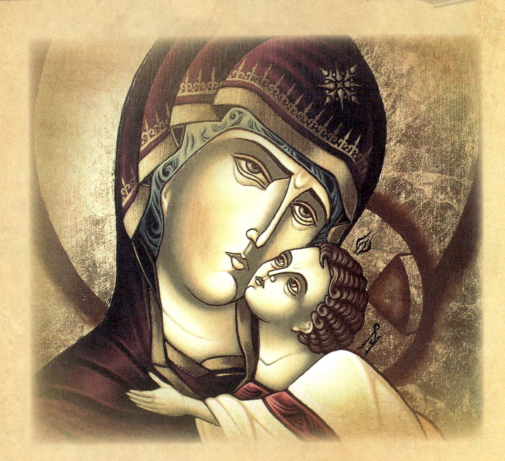

MARY AND
THE SAINTS

Session **9** MARY AND THE SAINTS

MARY AND THE SAINTS:
Our Spiritual Mother and the Communion of Saints

INTRODUCTION

For Catholics, Mary and the saints are important parts of daily life and devotion. Yet many outside the Church are confused as to what Catholics really believe. Do they worship Mary? Do they pray to the saints? And how does the saving action of Jesus fit into all of this?

Underlying everything the Church teaches about Mary and the saints is Jesus. The attention Catholics give to them does not distract from God, but enables us to draw into a more intimate communion with him, for just as fellowship with our Christian brothers and sisters on earth draws us closer to Jesus, so our communion with Mary and the saints draws us closer to him as well. Devotion to Mary and the saints is one way that Catholics come to know and love God and more deeply appreciate the great gift of salvation.

THIS SESSION WILL COVER:

- **The four basic dogmas the Church teaches about Mary**
- **How Jesus is at the heart of everything Catholics believe about Mary**
- **Why Catholics don't worship Mary and the saints, but honor them as models for all Christians**
- **What Catholics really mean when they say they "pray to" Mary and the saints**
- **Why Mary is the "Queen of Heaven"**
- **The mysteries of the Rosary**
- **What role Mary should play in the life of every believer**

Cover Photo Credit, Photo Credit: Mother of God © Iosif Chezan/shutterstock.com

Session 9 MARY AND THE SAINTS

OPENING PRAYER

Hail Mary, full of grace.
The Lord is with thee.
Blessed art thou amongst women,
and blessed is the fruit
of thy womb, Jesus.
Holy Mary, Mother of God,
pray for us sinners,
now and at the hour of our death.
Amen.

"Never be afraid of loving the Blessed Virgin too much. You can never love her more than Jesus did."
—St. Maximilian Kolbe

DISCUSSION QUESTIONS

1. Why do Catholics honor the saints?
   Why are the saints' prayers for us so powerful?

2. What are the four Catholic dogmas about Mary?
   What do they teach us about Jesus and the Father's plan of salvation?

3. How is Jesus's command to St. John to "Behold your mother" a challenge to us in our own prayer life and journey with Jesus?

Photo Credit: Mary praying © Bogdan Vasilescu/Shutterstock.com

Session **9** MARY AND THE SAINTS

CALL TO CONVERSION

After spending a few moments in prayer, write down your thoughts and reflections on the following questions:

#1 Reflect on the following words from St. Louis Marie de Montfort:

> "We never give more honor to Jesus than when we honor his Mother, and we honor her simply and solely to honor him all the more perfectly. We go to her only as a way leading to the goal we seek—Jesus, her Son."

Consider the four dogmas you learned about Mary in this week's lesson. How can accepting those teachings bring you to a deeper understanding of Jesus and his love for you?

_____
_____
_____
_____
_____
_____
_____

#2 At the end of the video, the presenter talked about who Mary is and what it means to develop a relationship with her. Take a few minutes to ask yourself what your relationship with Mary is like, and what you would like it to be. Ask God in prayer what keeps you from developing a closer relationship with Mary.

_____
_____
_____
_____
_____
_____
_____
_____

#3 There are many prayers and devotions in the Church dedicated to Mary, with the most prominent one being the Rosary. Take some time this week either to pray a Rosary if you are familiar with the prayer, or to learn more about how to pray a Rosary. As you do, reflect on how each mystery of the Rosary points us to Christ through Mary.

_____
_____
_____
_____
_____
_____

CLOSING PRAYER

The Memorare

Remember,
O most gracious Virgin Mary,
that never was it known
that anyone who fled to thy protection,
implored thy help
or sought thy intercession,
was left unaided.
Inspired by this confidence,
we fly unto thee,
O Virgin of virgins our Mother;
to thee do we come,
before thee we stand,
sinful and sorrowful;
O Mother of the Word Incarnate,
despise not our petitions,
but in thy mercy hear and answer us.
Amen.

Photo Credit: Coronation of the Virgin © RMN-Grand Palais / Art Resource, NY

Session 9 MARY AND THE SAINTS

SCRIPTURE VERSE FOR THE WEEK

Here is a verse from the Bible that you can memorize and reflect on this week to help you apply today's session to your daily life:

 "My soul glorifies the Lord and my spirit rejoices in God my Savior, for he has been mindful of the humble state of his servant." —Luke 1:47–48

BEHOLD, YOUR MOTHER

TO ENRICH YOUR CATHOLIC FAITH, VISIT FORMED.org

Where you'll find helpful videos, audio presentations, and ebooks from the most trustworthy presenters in the Catholic world.

For Further Reading:

For more in-depth reading about Mary and the Saints, see the following *Catechism* passages:

- *Immaculate Conception: CCC 490–493*
- *Mother of God: CCC 495*
- *Perpetual Virginity: CCC 496–500*
- *Assumption: CCC 966*
- *Devotion to Mary: CCC 971*

Other Resources:

- *United States Catholic Catechism for Adults*, **Chapter 12**
- *Apostolic Letter on the Rosary of the Blessed Virgin Mary, Rosarium Virginis Mariae* **by John Paul II**
- *The New Rosary in Scripture: Biblical Insights for Praying the 20 Mysteries* **by Dr. Edward Sri**
- *Butler's Lives of the Saints* **by Alban Butler**
- *Hail, Holy Queen: The Mother of God in the Word of God* **by Scott Hahn**
- *365 Saints* **by Woodeene Koenig-Bricker**

Session 10

THE LAST THINGS

Session 10 THE LAST THINGS

THE LAST THINGS:
What Happens After We Die?

INTRODUCTION

At some point in our lives we all wonder what will happen after we die. Of course, none of us can know exactly what will occur—despite the numerous books written about near-death experiences—but as Christians we have One Who Has Gone Before Us in the Person of Jesus, whose Death and Resurrection shed light on what awaits us. He has given us some indication of what awaits, and the Church has continued to help us with her instruction.

The Church teaches that if we are to grow and mature as Christians, we need to take time to prayerfully consider the Four Last Things—death, judgment, Heaven, and Hell. Unless and until we take these things seriously, our life here on earth will lack meaning and focus. It's only when we consider the decisions we make in the light of eternity that our entire lives begin to make sense and our relationship with God can come to full maturity.

THIS SESSION WILL COVER:

- **The Particular Judgment of each soul at the moment of death**
- **Hell: what it is, and why, if we fail to repent, we will be separated from God forever**
- **Heaven, the perfect communion of life and love with the Trinity**
- **Purgatory, the purification some need before entering into full communion with God**
- **Why Catholics pray for the dead**

Cover Photo Credit, Photo Credit: Tombstone © Stuart Monk/shutterstock.com

Session 10 THE LAST THINGS

OPENING PRAYER

A Prayer for a Happy Death

Lord Jesus Christ,
who willest that no man should perish,
and to whom supplication is never
made without the hope of mercy,
for Thou saidst
with Thine Own holy and blessed lips:
"All things whatsoever ye shall ask in My name,
shall be done unto you";
I ask of Thee, O Lord,
for Thy holy Name's sake,
to grant me at the hour of my death
full consciousness and the power of speech,
sincere contrition for my sins,
true faith, firm hope and perfect charity,
that I may be able to say unto Thee with a clean heart:
Into Thy hands, O Lord, I commend my spirit:
Thou hast redeemed me, O God of truth,
who art blessed forever and ever. Amen.
—St. Vincent Ferrer

> *"O my dear parishioners, let us endeavor to get to heaven! There we shall see God. How happy we shall feel! We must get to heaven! What a pity it would be if some of you were to find yourselves on the other side!"*
> —St. John Vianney

DISCUSSION QUESTIONS

1. We all have various images of Heaven, but according to the video, what is Heaven?

2. In the presentation, the Catholic teaching on Purgatory is discussed. What are some of the misconceptions about Purgatory? What does the Catholic Church really teach about Purgatory? And why can Purgatory be seen, at least in some sense, as something for which we should be grateful?

3. Why is it accurate to state, "God doesn't send people to Hell"?

CALL TO CONVERSION

After spending a few moments in prayer, write down your thoughts and reflections on the following questions:

#1 In the words of a traditional Catechism, "God made us to know him, to love him, and to serve him in this world, and to be happy with him forever in heaven." As we go through our lives, the single most important question we need to ask in light of eternity is *How can we know, love, and serve God?* If we want our lives on earth to have meaning, we need to explore this question in depth. What do you think it means to know God? What does it mean to love God? What does it mean to serve God? What is one way this week that you can get to know God better? To love him more deeply? To serve him more completely? Ask the Holy Spirit for guidance—and courage—to follow through on your commitment.

___
___
___
___
___

Session **10** THE LAST THINGS

#2 Reflect on the following quote from the Ash Wednesday liturgy: "Remember, man, that you are dust and to dust you shall return." How does this quote make you feel? Why do you think that the Church asks us to reflect on this statement at the beginning of Lent? How might this prayer help you focus more on what is truly important in this life?

___

#3 At the end of the presentation, Dr. Sri asks a fundamental question: "Are you moving toward eternity with Jesus or without him?" Take some time to look over your life, your priorities, the way you spend your days. Is your life moving toward Jesus or away from him? How would your life be different if you were truly making all your decisions in the light of your eternal destiny?

___

Session 10 THE LAST THINGS

CLOSING PRAYER

St. Alphonsus Liguori's Night Prayer

Jesus Christ, my God,
I adore you and thank you
for all the graces
you have given me this day.
I offer you my sleep
and all the moments of this night,
and I beg of you to keep me without sin.
Therefore, I put myself
within your sacred side
and under the mantle of our lady,
my Mother.
Let your holy angels
stand about me and keep me in peace;
and let your blessing be upon me.
Amen.

Photo Credit: The descent to limbo / Erich Lessing / Art Resource, NY

Session 10 THE LAST THINGS

SCRIPTURE VERSE FOR THE WEEK

Here is a verse from the Bible that you can memorize and reflect on this week to help you apply today's session to your daily life:

 "And just as it is appointed for man to die once, and after that comes judgment." —Hebrews 9:27

LIVING TODAY FOR ETERNITY

TO ENRICH YOUR CATHOLIC FAITH, VISIT FORMED.org

Where you'll find helpful videos, audio presentations, and ebooks from the most trustworthy presenters in the Catholic world.

For Further Reading:

For more in-depth reading about the Last Things see the following *Catechism* passages:

- *Particular Judgment: CCC 1021–1022*
- *Heaven: CCC 1023–1029*
- *Hell: CCC 1033–1037*
- *Purgatory: CCC 1030–1032*
- *Last Judgment: CCC 1038–1041*

Other Resources:

- *United States Catholic Catechism for Adults,* **Chapter 13**
- *The Last Things* **by Regis Martin**
- *Heaven, the Heart's Deepest Longing* **by Peter Kreeft**
- *Encyclical Letter, Saved by Hope* **by Pope Benedict XVI** (www.vatican.va/holy_father/benedict_xvi/encyclicals/documents/hf_ben-xvi_enc_20071130_spe-salvi_en.html)

NOTES

FROM THE AUGUSTINE INSTITUTE GRADUATE SCHOOL OF THEOLOGY

Short Courses
Certification and Enrichment for Catholics

Study Catholic theology online. Develop a deeper understanding of your Catholic Faith with engaging curriculum designed and taught by the Augustine Institute faculty. Earn your certificate in Catholic Theology at the conclusion of the nine-course core curriculum. Each Short Course includes

- Three hours of high-quality video instruction
- Detailed companion presentation slides
- Reading assignments that are modest in length but generous in depth and beauty
- Quizzes to guide your learning
- Related resources: books, video, audio, and more

Learn more at
AugustineInstitute.org/ShortCourses

AUGUSTINE INSTITUTE®
GRADUATE SCHOOL OF THEOLOGY

It's not about what it is.
It's about *Who* it is.

Prepare yourself and your family to receive Jesus in the Eucharist as never before with *Presence: The Mystery of the Eucharist*. World-renowned Catholic presenters unveil the truth and beauty behind the "source and summit" of the Christian life, from its origins in Sacred Scripture, to its profound role in the life of the Church and its members.

Learn more at AugustineInstitute.org/Presence

Presence
THE MYSTERY OF THE EUCHARIST

AUGUSTINE INSTITUTE